Citizenship and PSHE
Book 1

Contents

Deena Haydon
Pat King
Christine Moorcroft

Personal development

Jack and Sabrina chose what they wanted to have in their pictures. They chose things that are important to them.

Jack

Sabrina

1. Talk to a partner about what is important to Jack and Sabrina.

2. List the important things you would put in your picture.

Make a table.

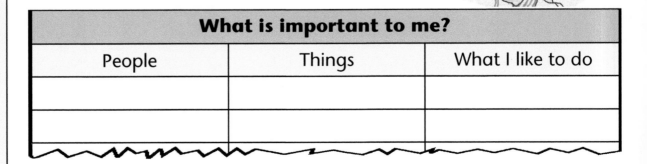

Talk about important people and important things.

What is important to me?		
People	Things	What I like to do

3. Interview a partner about something that is important to him or her.

> You could ask:
>
> – Where did it come from?
> – How long have you had it?
> – Does it remind you of anything or anyone?

We are all special.

4. Think of three things that make the person next to you special. Tell him or her.
What does he or she think?

5. Make a badge or a certificate to show why you are special.

What makes a person special? Everyone is special in some way.

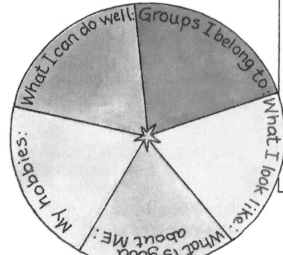

1. With a partner, talk about all the things you notice about the children in the picture.

Think about age, hair colour and style, skin colour, height and other similarities and differences.

2. Think of six of your own features. How many others in the class have the same features?

Make a table.

Is anyone exactly like you?

Feature	Me	Others
brown hair		
grey eyes		

3. Draw a person with short brown hair, blue eyes, long black eyelashes, brown eyebrows, a smiling mouth, a long straight nose and pierced ears.

4. Make a display of all the pictures made by your group. How are the pictures the same? How are they different?

Some have straight hair.

This one has freckles and thin lips.

Think about things like kindness, sense of humour and honesty.

People may have similar features but still look very different.
They can be different in other ways.

Some similarities and differences cannot be seen.

5. With a partner, list some of the characteristics that do not show on pictures or photographs.

Make a table.

Characteristic	What the person does
kindness	Helps. Comforts people who are upset. Shares things.
sense of humour	

I wanna be a star.
I wanna go far.
I wanna drive around
in a big red car.

From
I Wanna be a Star
by Tony Mitton

1. Talk to a partner about what
Stella wants to do.
How could she do it?
How easy would it be?
How much might it cost?

What talents
might Stella need?
What might she need
to learn?
Will she need to save
up?

2. List all the things you would like
to be able to do.

3. When might you be able to do the
things you want to do?

In a few weeks
Stop fighting with my sister.
Bowl a cricket ball.

Next year
Play the recorder.
Count to 100 in French.

When I am ten
Draw good pictures of horses.

When I am grown up
Drive a car.

Never!
Be invisible whenever I want to.

4. Choose one of the things you might be able to do in a few weeks' time.
That is your target.

I want to be good at catching a ball.

You can catch a big ball.

I want to be able to catch a tennis ball.

5. Write down your target.
With a partner, decide what you can already do towards your target.

6. Decide exactly what you will be able to do when you reach your target.
Write a plan for reaching your target.

My target	To catch eight out of every ten tennis balls thrown to me.
My plan	I shall practise catching a tennis ball for 15 minutes each day.

My target	To stop fighting with my sister.
My plan	On a calendar, I shall put a star on each day when I don't fight with her.

What can you do to help reach your targets?

The work people do

People need different abilities for different jobs.
They need to learn different things.
Sometimes personal qualities are important.

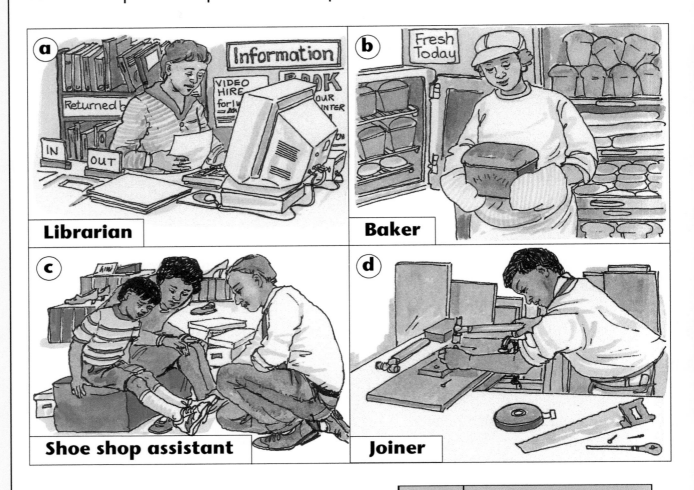

a Librarian

b Baker

c Shoe shop assistant

d Joiner

1. What do the people in the pictures do at work?

Draw a chart.

Jobs	What they do
a	
b	

2. With a partner, list the abilities each person needs to do that job well.

Think of abilities like listening to people, remembering, and working with materials.

Mark is a receptionist.
He has to make people feel welcome.
He has to be friendly and polite.

3. If you were a receptionist at your school, what would you do to:
- welcome people
- be friendly
- be polite?

4. List the jobs that children do in your school. Which of these jobs would you be good at?

5. Make up an application form for one of those jobs.

6. Fill it in. Say why you would be good at that job.

I would be a good tuck-shop monitor because I am good at adding up money.

I would be a good lunch-table leader because I like looking after younger children in the school.

What have you learned about the abilities people need for their work?

Citizenship

1. Can you see anyone doing something wrong in this picture?

2. In a group, talk about what is happening and why.

3. Make a table.

Event	Reasons
Breaking a fence	They think it is funny. They don't think it matters if you damage property. They … .
Teenagers fighting	

4. Make a list of things people do that you think are wrong.

I think it's wrong to cheat in a game.

I think it's wrong to harm people or their property.

I think it's wrong to steal.

Why are these things wrong?

Why do you think people do these things or behave in these ways?

Think about: causing harm, upsetting others, breaking rules and being dishonest.

Make a table.

Word bank	**Things that are wrong**	**Why they are wrong**	**Why people do them**
accident	Cheating		
attention-seeking			
easily influenced			
hungry			
persuaded			
poor			
showing off			
unaware of others			
uncaring			

What should we do?

5. What do you think Kathryn and Mahesh should do?

Does everyone agree about what is right and wrong?

1. Why did the children want to play without rules?

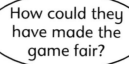
How could they have made the game fair?

2. Did they all enjoy the game? Do you think the winners and losers felt the same way?

a

b

c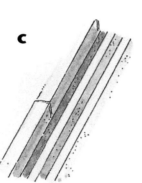

d

e

3. These signs show rules for the road. Find out what they mean. Why are they needed?

Make a table.

Sign	Meaning	Why needed
a		
b		

Swimming pool rules

4. List some rules for another place or situation.

5. Why do we have rules?

Think about safety, protection from harm and fairness.

6. What might happen if there were no rules?

In what ways are rules important?

Responsibilities

1. What are 'responsibilities'?
What do you have responsibility for?

 I am responsible for my own behaviour.

We are all responsible for helping to keep our school tidy.

2. Some responsibilities are actions or types of behaviour that are important for you to carry out.

Draw and describe three responsibilities you have.

Do you have any special jobs?

Do you care for a person, animal or equipment?

Think about responsibilities at home and school.

Do you behave in certain ways?

Do you follow instructions?

Some responsibilities are actions or types of behaviour carried out by you as part of a group.

Groups you belong to may include: family, class, school, club, audience or community

I didn't hear that. What do we have to do?

They all knew it was Sara who tripped me up, but Miss just thinks I'm telling tales.

Oh no! I don't know how the story ends because the last page has been torn out.

3. Make a table showing what responsibilities the children in this classroom share. Add two other shared responsibilities.

Responsibility	Why everyone shares this responsibility
To listen when someone speaks.	

4. Draw a time line showing your responsibilities at different ages.
Are any the same for all ages?

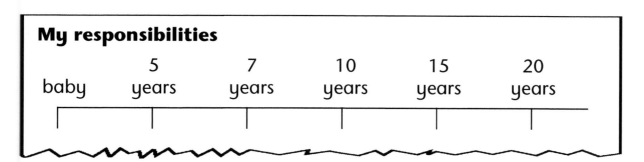

My responsibilities

baby	5 years	7 years	10 years	15 years	20 years

Communities

A community is a place where people live together.
This picture shows parts of a community.

 1. Think why each of these buildings is useful to people in a community.

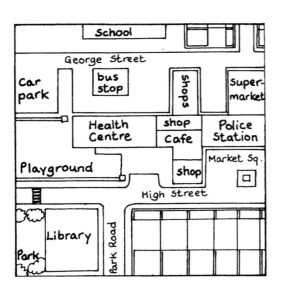

Place	Why it is useful
school	
shops	
library	

 2. In a group, find or draw a map of your local area. Mark the useful buildings on your map. Design a key.

Some people are paid to do jobs that help the community.

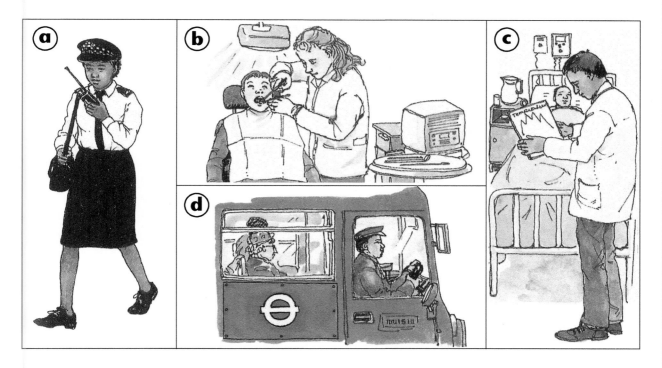

3. How do these people help the community? Make a table.
Think of people who help your community and add them to your table.

Picture	Job	Help for the community
a	police officer	
b		

4. People who live near to each other are neighbours. Make a list of your neighbours.

I feed my neighbours' cat when they are on holiday.

5. How can neighbours help each other?

We kept our neighbour company when he was ill.

How could you help people in your community?

17

1. What kind of problem might Usha have?
Who might she be talking to?

2. Everyone has problems or needs help at some time.
It often helps to talk about how we feel.

Who could these children talk to?
How might this help?

3. Does everyone have someone
they can talk to?

4. Some people work for groups that have been set up to listen to, or help, other people.
Find out about voluntary groups and charities in your community.

Make a table.

You could invite in a volunteer to explain what they do and find out more about their work.

Voluntary group or charity	What it does	Who it is for	Where it is in our community

5. Design an information leaflet for one of the voluntary groups or charities in your table.

Does your group:
- raise money
- provide help or support
- provide information
- train people to listen or help
- help people to understand how others live and feel?

How could you support a local charity?

19

Our environment

Our environment is where we live.

1. Which of these places is most like where you live?

2. Talk to a partner about the pictures and about where you live.

What is good about the place where you live?

What might be good about the other places?

3. What might be not so good about each place? Working in a group, list as many things as you can.

Make a table.

Place	Good points	Bad points
a		

Think about what it looks like, smell, noise, people, shops, transport, things to do and space.

4. Draw and describe a place where you would like to live. What is good about it?

 5. Sometimes people spoil the place where they live.
In a group, talk about how these places have been
spoiled.

Think about why people
do these things.
Share your ideas with
the class.

 6. List things that spoil
where you live.

Make a table.

Things that spoil where I live	How they spoil it

Word bank

dumping	pollution
fumes	rubbish
graffiti	smell
noise	vandalism

 7. Choose one of the things on
your list.
Make a poster persuading
people not to do it.

What could you do to look after your environment?

Lifestyle

1. Which of these pictures shows someone about the same age as you?

2. You used to be like some of the others.
What were you like when you were younger?
Make a table.

Age	What I looked like	What I could do	What I could not do
When I was born			
1			
3			
5			

3. Continue the chart to show what you are like now.

4. Think about important things that have happened to you.
Draw a time line to show them.

This is Gwenan's time line.

I was born. | I went into hospital. | My baby sister was born. | I went to playgroup. | I started school. | I went to Disneyland.

5. What was better about being younger?
What is better about being your age?

6. Talk to your group about who looked after you when you were younger. What did they do for you?

7. Think about something or someone you look after.
What do you do?

8. Draw and write some instructions for looking after something or somebody.

What have been the most important changes in your life?

Dangerous places

Homes can be dangerous places.

1. List the dangers in these pictures.

Dangers	
Picture a	Picture b

As safe as houses!?

2. Draw another part of the house in the picture, such as a living room, hall or bathroom. Include some dangers in your drawing.
Ask a partner to list the dangers in your picture.
Redraw one of the pictures, but this time make it safe.
Label what you have changed.

Think about things that are dangerous to touch, taste, smell, or may cause an accident.

3. Collect pictures of things that can harm you at home.
Explain how they can be kept safe.

Signs in the environment help us to keep safe.
How do these signs help us?

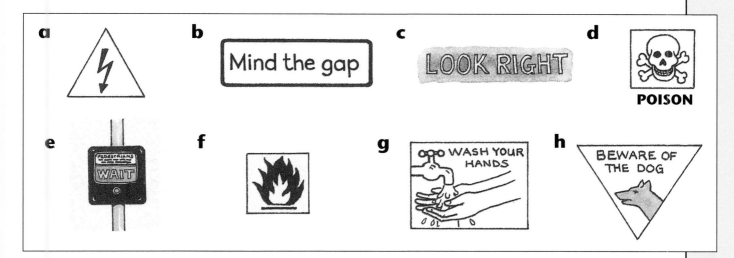

4. Copy and complete the table.

Sign	What it tells us	How it keeps us safe
a		
b		

5. Draw any safety signs that you have seen at home, at school or out and about.

Signs tell us things by their shape and colour.

6. Match the instructions to these road sign outlines.

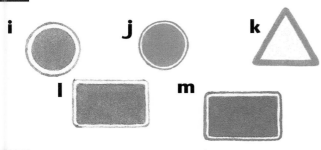

Meaning	Sign
Do something	
Do not do something	
Information	
Warning	
Instruction	

7. Design some signs to use in your school.

What can you do to make sure you are safe at home, at school or out and about?

Harmful materials

Some materials that can harm us are safe when used properly.

hairspray

bleach

strong glue

paintbrush cleaner

powder paint

1. For what should the materials be used?
Who should use them?

Copy and complete the table.

Material	Purpose	Who should use it?
bleach		
strong glue		

2. Find out how people protect themselves and others when they use these materials.

Add other everyday materials that can harm people.

Drugs change the ways in which our minds and bodies work.
When we are ill drugs (medicines) can help.

Jenny has asthma.
She uses an inhaler.

3. Which pictures show when drugs are safe?
Make a table.

Picture	Safe or unsafe
a	
b	

4. Some medicines stop us becoming ill. Some help our bodies fight illness.
Some stop us feeling pain.
Some help us cope with illness.

 Only take medicine from an adult you trust.

In a group, think of an example of each kind of medicine.
Who might need them?

5. What medicines do you know?
With a partner, draw and list them and show what they are for.

Medicine	What it is for
aspirin	
insulin	

How can you make sure that materials do not harm you?

Help!

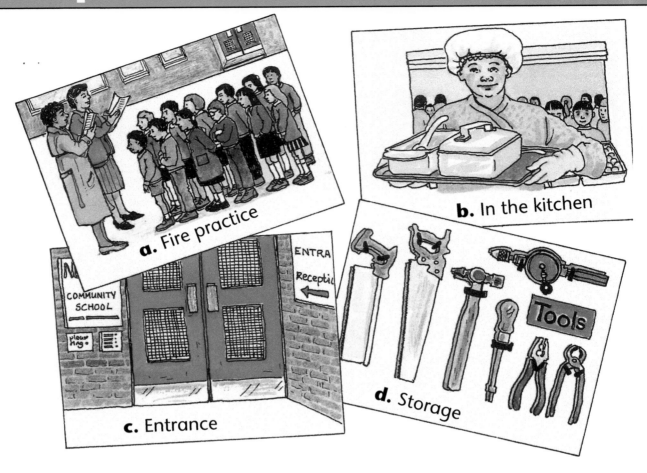

a. Fire practice

b. In the kitchen

c. Entrance

d. Storage

1. Talk to a partner about the pictures.

Copy and complete the table.

Picture	Risk	How people stay safe
a	Fire	They know what to do if there is a fire.
b	Germs	

What is the risk?

How do people protect themselves from it?

2. Find out how your school helps you to stay safe and healthy.

Karl's grandad is ill.
He has a pain in his chest. He has trouble breathing.
There are no other adults at home.
Karl has to telephone for help.

3. What telephone number should Karl use? Which emergency service will he need? What information will he need to give?

Emergency services are ambulance, fire, police and coastguard.

Think about the questions Karl will be asked.

4. Sometimes people call emergency services when they do not need them.

With a partner, list all the problems this can cause.

Think about problems for the emergency services, people who are ill, badly hurt, or in danger.

What would you do in an emergency?

29

Safe choices

Sometimes it is difficult to make safe choices.

1. With a partner, draw and write three different endings for this story:

2. Did the girls think about what might happen to them? How can you tell?

Make a table.

Think about what they said.

Name	Did she think about the dangers?	How I can tell
Becky		
Kim		

3. What might have influenced the girls' choices?

4. Make notes about a difficult choice you once made.
Describe the things that influenced you.

Think about excitement, fun and persuasion.

These children are doing dangerous things for different reasons.

Emma knows that matches are dangerous.

Dan knows that he should check for traffic before crossing a road.

Emma and Dan were lucky. They did not get hurt.

5. Why did Emma ignore what she knew?
Why did Dan ignore what he knew?

6. In a group, list other risky choices that children make.
Make up a play that will help younger children to make safe choices.

Think about deep water, electricity, railways, strangers and climbing.

What helps you to make safe choices?

Things that influence us

Advertisements often try to persuade people to do things, go to places or buy things.

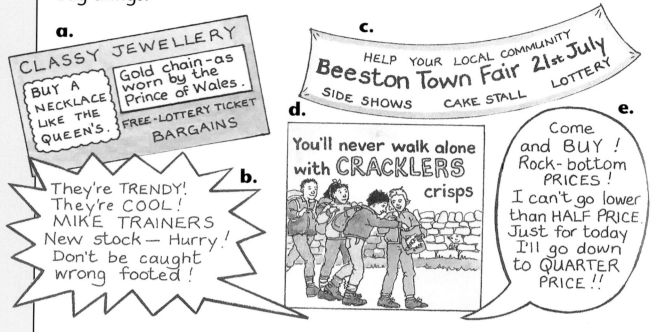

a. CLASSY JEWELLERY
BUY A NECKLACE LIKE THE QUEEN'S.
Gold chain – as worn by the Prince of Wales.
FREE – LOTTERY TICKET
BARGAINS

b. They're TRENDY! They're COOL! MIKE TRAINERS New stock — Hurry! Don't be caught wrong footed!

c. HELP YOUR LOCAL COMMUNITY
Beeston Town Fair 21st July
SIDE SHOWS   CAKE STALL   LOTTERY

d. You'll never walk alone with CRACKLERS crisps

e. Come and BUY! Rock-bottom PRICES! I can't go lower than HALF PRICE. Just for today I'll go down to QUARTER PRICE!!

1. What do these advertisements try to persuade people to do? How do they do this?

Make a table.

Advertisement	What it advertises	How it tries to persuade
a		
b		

Here are some ideas to help you: trendy, makes you popular, a bargain, last chance, like rich people, you will be doing good, you may win money.

2. Look for other advertisements in newspapers, magazines, on the Internet and on television. Listen to radio advertisements. Use the table to describe them.

3. List some things that you or your family have done or bought after seeing or hearing advertisements.

4. What does this advertisement tell you about Fun Fruiteez?

5. Design an advertisement that tells everything about *Fun Fruiteez*. Write a jingle to go with it.

Advertisements are not the only persuaders.

6. In this picture, who is being persuaded?
- by whom?
- to do what?

7. Draw and describe what might happen next.

What influences you?

Togetherness

 1. How might the people in each photograph be related to one another? (For example, mother, father.)

Think about: being related, family names.

 2. Draw your family. What do you call the people in your family?

Relationship words

aunt	foster-parent	husband	sister
brother	friend	mother	stepfather
carer	grandfather	nephew	stepmother
cousin	grandmother	niece	uncle
father	guardian	partner	wife

Relationships

Families may not all live together in the same house.
These pictures show people from the same family.

3. Describe the family in the pictures.

4. List the people in your
family who live with you
and those who do not
live with you.
Make a table.

My family	
Live with me	Do not live with me

Families have different ways of spending time together.
They have different ways of keeping in touch with one another.

5. How do you spend time with your family or keep in touch
with them?
Make a table.

I see these people			I phone these people	I write to these people
Every day	**Every week**	**Less often**		

What is a family?

35

What is a friend?

 1. How can you tell that these children are friends?

 2. Talk in a group. What is special about a good friend?
Share your ideas with the class.

 3. Write an advertisement describing the kind of friend you would like.

WANTED

Seven year old boy or girl who enjoys.....

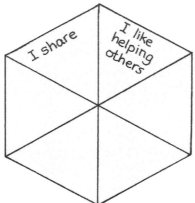

I share

I like helping others

 4. Would you be a good friend? Think of six qualities that make you a good friend.

 Copy and complete a friendship hexagon.

You may like doing some things together and some apart.

5. Draw two things you like doing with a friend.

When did you last tell your friends that you like them?

Friends may be like you or different from you.

6. Send a happigram to someone you care about.
It might be a friend, someone you want to be friends with or a member of your family.

Happigram
to ....
I'm glad you are my friend because....

Thank you for helping me with ....

I really enjoyed ....

7. How could you help someone who finds it hard to make friends?

Other people's feelings

_____ , _____ and _____ are together.

_____ is alone.

1. Draw each child with a thought bubble. Write down what they are feeling.

Word bank		
angry	excited	lonely
bored	happy	pleased
disappointed	left out	sad

2. Write down or draw what might have happened before the scene in the picture.

3. How might each child have felt before the scene in the picture?

Sam felt _____

Jodie felt _____

Chris felt _____

Robin felt_____

Share your ideas in a group. Decide how the children would feel.

4. What could the children in the picture do so that they would all feel good?

5. In your group, make a list of ways in which people can make others feel bad.

Think about what they could say or do.

Ignore her.

You're stupid.

Make a list of ways in which people can make others feel good.

Play with us.

She gave me a lovely smile.

6. Write each idea from your list on to the back of a smiling or sad face. Hang them up to make a mobile.

Call them names

share a toy

1. In each of these pictures, one child is upset.
In a group, decide why they are upset.
Think of words for how they might feel.

For each picture, what could a good friend do?

How can you tell when a friend is upset?

Sometimes friends can say unkind things or be bad-tempered.

 2. Draw a picture of you and a friend.

3. What might have made your friend behave like this? What could you do about it?

4. In a group, make a list of what a good friend will do. What will a good friend try not to do?

Make a table.

A good friend will	A good friend won't
be honest	tell you lies
listen to you	call you names

Arguments

1. In a group, list ways in which the people in this story could make it a sad ending.

List ways in which the people in this story could make it a happy ending.

Make a table.

Sad	Happy
Keep shouting	Calm down

2. Why do friends quarrel?
List five ways to stay friends after a quarrel.

I quarrelled with Colin. I could promise not to forget to call for him tomorrow.

Being rude can start a quarrel or argument.
Sometimes people in families quarrel.

I told you not to play with it.

I didn't mean to break it.

3. How could this child try to make up after the quarrel?
What could the adult do?

Say 'sorry' and really meaning it can sometimes be hard.

4. Copy and complete these sentences:

I find it easy to say 'sorry' when _____ .

I find it hard to say 'sorry' when _____ .

What could you do next time you quarrel with a friend?

Bullying

Carrie

Hannah

Suzi

 1. What is happening in this picture?

How does Suzi feel?

 In a group, think of words to describe how she feels.

How might Carrie and Hannah feel?

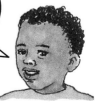

Think of different ways in which people are bullied.

2. Why might Carrie and Hannah be bullying Suzi?
List your ideas.
Share your ideas in a group.

They are just mean!

Suzi is not nice.

3. Imagine that you are in Suzi's class.
What could everyone do to help Suzi?

Suzi could ...

The other children could ...

I would tell Suzi to ...

I could help Suzi by ...

Put your ideas on separate pieces of paper.
Make a class display of support.

4. Write a letter to Carrie or Hannah, telling them what you think of their behaviour.
Finish by saying 'Why don't you ...'

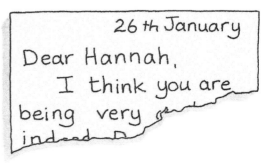

26th January

Dear Hannah,
I think you are being very ...
indeed ...

Different customs

People celebrate special events in different ways.

New Year in Scotland

Chinese New Year

Thanksgiving in the USA

British Harvest Festival

1. What are people celebrating in each of these pictures?

What do people do when they celebrate?

Think about special food, gifts and words.

Think about special music, clothing and places.

2. In a group, find out how people in a range of cultures or countries celebrate harvest and New Year.

Find out how different cultures and countries celebrate other special events.

Think about celebrating births, birthdays, religious festivals, special events in history.

In the UK, people have bonfires and fireworks on the 5th of November because ... .

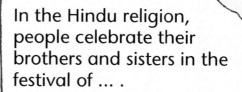

In the Hindu religion, people celebrate their brothers and sisters in the festival of ... .

3. In a group, write about some of the things you have found out about.

4. Make a display and explain the customs to the class.

5. Sometimes, families have their own special celebrations. Write about special events in your family.

When I lost my tooth, my Dad ... .

My Gran and Grandad had a special wedding anniversary and we all ... .

Why is it good to have different customs?

Glossary

abilities (8)	Things that somebody can do.
accident (11, 24)	Something that is not meant to happen.
anniversary (47)	A day (or time) when people remember or celebrate an event. An anniversary is a number of years.
application form (9)	A form filled in to ask for something, such as a ticket for an event, or a job.
asthma (27)	A disease that can make breathing difficult.
attention-seeking (11)	Trying to make someone notice you.
auntie (34)	Mother's or father's sister.
carer (34)	Someone who looks after a person who needs help.
charity (19)	An organisation created to help people.
cheat (11)	Trick or be untruthful.
community (16)	A place where people live together.
cousin (34)	Son or daughter of an **uncle** or **aunt**.
custom (46)	A usual way of behaving for a person or group of people.
dishonest (11)	Not truthful.
drug (27)	A material used as a **medicine**, to cure or prevent illness or as a painkiller. A material that some people take to alter their state of mind.
emergency (29)	An event that needs immediate action.
environment (20, 25)	The place around you.
fair (13)	Being honest or keeping to rules.
features (4)	Parts of the face: for example, the nose and eyes.
graffiti (21)	Drawings or writings on things such as buildings or walls.
guardian (34)	Someone who is in charge of a child instead of his or her mother or father.
influence (30)	Things or people trying to make you do or behave in certain ways, make certain choices or believe certain things.
medicine (27)	A **drug** used to prevent or cure illness or as a painkiller.
neighbour (17)	A person who lives nearby.
nephew (34)	Son of a brother or sister.
niece (34)	Daughter of a brother or sister.
persuade (21, 32)	To try to make a person believe or do something.
pollution (21)	Harm to the environment, for example, by making it dirty.
property (11)	Something owned by someone.
responsibility (14)	An action or way of behaving that is important for a person to carry out.
rule (12)	An agreed way of behaving or doing things.
unaware (11)	Not noticing something or somebody.
uncle (34)	Mother's or father's brother.
vandalism (21)	Damage done on purpose to things or places.
voluntary group (19)	A group of people who do things for which they are not paid.